Extreme Snowboarding

by Pat Ryan

Content Consultant:

Don Sather

United States of America Snowboard Association

(USASA)

CAPSTONE PRESS

MANKATO, MINNESOTA

C A P S T O N E   P R E S S

818 North Willow Street • Mankato, Minnesota 56001
http://www.capstone-press.com

Printed in the United States of America.

Library of Congress Cataloging-in-Publication Data
Ryan, Pat.
    Extreme snowboarding/by Pat Ryan.
    p. cm. -- (Extreme sports)
    Includes bibliographical references and index.
    Summary: Describes the history, equipment, personalities, and contemporary practice of extreme snowboarding.
    ISBN 1-56065-536-4
    1. Snowboarding--Juvenile literature. [1. Snowboarding.]
    I. Title. II. Series
GV857.S57R93 1998
796.9--dc21

                                              97-11339
                                                 CIP
                                                  AC

Editorial credits
Editor, Timothy Larson; Cover design, Timothy Halldin; Photo Research Assistant, Michelle L. Norstad
Photo credits
Images International/Erwin C. "Bud" Nielson, 14, 22, 30, 47
Int'l Stock/Eric Sanford, 24, 32
Gallup Photography, Inc./Mark Gallup, 18
MSI/Richard Cheski, cover, 4, 6, 9, 16, 26, 28, 34, 36, 38, 40
Unicorn Stock/Jim Shippe, 10; Dick Young, 12; Dave Lyons, 20

Table of Contents

Chapter 1
Snowboarding

Snowboarding is the sport of riding a snowboard downhill over snow. A snowboard looks like a large snow ski. A person who snowboards is called a snowboarder. Boarder is a shortened word for snowboarder. A boarder stands on a snowboard and rides it down a slope.

Snowboarding takes place on ski slopes or at snow parks. A snow park is a part of a ski area set aside for snowboarders. A snow park has special courses built into the snow just for snowboarding.

There is amateur and professional snowboarding. Professional snowboarding has a high level of difficulty. Professional boarders have a high level of skill. They also receive money for taking part in the sport. Amateur snowboarding is not as difficult as professional snowboarding. Amateur boarders take part in snowboarding only for pleasure.

Snowboarding is the sport of riding a snowboard downhill over snow.

Some snowboarders prefer to snowboard in the backcountry.

Extreme Snowboarding

Professional snowboarding is called extreme
snowboarding. There are four basic kinds of extreme
snowboarding. The first kind takes place at snow
parks. This is called slope-style snowboarding. Slope-
style snowboarders show their skill by doing tricks.

The second kind of extreme snowboarding is
downhill. In extreme downhill races, boarders race
down long courses. The courses are built on steep ski

slopes. Boarders try to finish the courses in the shortest times.

Wind snowboarding is the third and newest kind of extreme snowboarding. The idea for wind snowboarding came from windsurfing. Snowboarders saw that they could add sails to their snowboards like the sails on windsurfing boards.

In wind snowboarding, sails on snowboards catch the wind. This pushes wind boarders down slopes. The sails also let boarders ride their boards uphill. On a good ride, boarders can make it all the way up a slope. Wind snowboarders use ski areas and backcountry areas.

Extreme Backcountry

Some extreme boarders prefer the fourth kind of extreme snowboarding. They like to snowboard on their own in the backcountry. Backcountry is rough or untouched hill or mountain areas where few people have been. This is called extreme backcountry snowboarding. Backcountry boarders are known for their ability to snowboard on unmarked slopes.

Extreme boarders go to the backcountry to find fresh, soft snow called powder. They think powder is the best snow for snowboarding. Many extreme boarders go to the mountains to find the freshest powder and the steepest slopes.

Boarders hike up mountains to find powder and steep slopes. Sometimes they ride up mountains in Snowcats. A Snowcat is a truck made to operate in the snow. Other times, boarders fly up mountains in helicopters. A helicopter is an aircraft with large turning blades on top.

The Extreme Boarder

Extreme boarders are athletes who work hard to be their best. An athlete is someone trained in a sport or game. Boarders always try to improve their skills and perform the best tricks. They practice and master skills. They experiment with new skills and tricks. Boarders also exercise to improve the condition of their bodies.

Extreme boarders learn and practice other skills along with their snowboarding skills. Boarders must be aware of danger and stay in

Extreme boarders go to the backcountry to find fresh, soft snow called powder.

control. For example, boarders learn how to deal with rocks buried in the snow. They also must be able to handle steep mountain cliffs and dangerous drop-offs. Dangerous means likely to cause harm.

Chapter 2

History of Snowboarding

Snowboarding began in the mid-1960s when Sherman Poppen invented the first snowboard. Poppen created the board for his daughter. He made his board by screwing two snow skis together with wooden pegs. His daughter stood on the sled and rode it down snow hills.

Poppen's wife called the sled the Snurfer. She created the name by combining the words snow and surfer. She saw that her daughter rode the snow sled like a surfer rides a surfboard.

Other children saw the Snurfer and they each wanted one. Poppen built Snurfers for them. Then he made Snurfers to sell to people. His sled gave inventors their ideas for the first one-piece snowboards.

Snowboards

Inventors like Tom Sims and Jake Burton improved Poppen's Snurfer. They called their inventions

Inventors of one-pieced snowboards like these were inspired by Sherman Poppen's Snurfer.

Skiers thought snowboarders tore up ski slopes.

snowboards. The men made one-piece boards shaped like large snow skis. This is the shape of today's snowboards.

The two men kept improving their snowboards. They tested the boards to see which were the easiest to ride. Today, Sims owns Sims Snowboards. Burton owns Burton Snowboards.

Shredders

There were only several thousand snowboarders until the early 1980s. Boarders usually snowboarded for fun. Many of the first boarders were surfers and skateboarders. They snowboarded when it was too cold to surf or skateboard. They discovered that boarding was fun and challenging.

Early boarders snowboarded on ski slopes. This caused problems between skiers and boarders. The skiers did not understand snowboarding. They did not believe that snowboarding was a serious sport. Skiers also thought snowboarders tore up ski slopes. They called boarders shredders for this reason.

Boarders decided to search for their own areas. They put on snowshoes and hiked up mountains. The boarders found private areas to snowboard in the backcountry.

Early Competition

Soon, boarders set up snowboard competitions. A competition is a contest between two or more athletes. The competitions helped the boarders show off and improve their skills.

Competitions showed skiers and the world that snowboarding was a serious sport. Thousands of people all over the world began snowboarding. They set up snowboarding groups and clubs.

Boarders and snowboarding fans soon wanted to see professionals compete. In 1983, sponsors helped boarders hold the first World Snowboarding Championship. A sponsor is a person or business that helps organize and pay for an event.

Chapter 3

Extreme Competition

Today's extreme snowboarding competitions feature freestyle events and downhill events. Freestyle events include half-pipe and slope-style riding. Boarders compete on special courses at snow parks. In freestyle events, boarders try to do the best tricks.

Downhill events feature races on courses built along steep mountain slopes. Downhill events include speed and slalom races. In downhill events, boarders try to complete a course in the fastest time.

Half-Pipe and Slope-Style Riding

In half-pipe riding, boarders ride their boards on a half-pipe. A half-pipe is a U-shaped course with high walls and rounded sides. A half-pipe course looks like half of a large pipe. Boarders race up and down the sides of a half-pipe course.

A half-pipe course has high walls and rounded sides.

Boarders race in and out between poles in a slalom race.

Boarders also do tricks as they race through a half-pipe. Many half-pipe tricks are aerials. An aerial is a trick done in midair. Half-pipe tricks include ollies, tailgrabs, and fakies.

An ollie is a jump into the air. A tailgrab is when a boarder grabs the end of the board. A fakie is turning around to face the opposite direction while boarding. Boarders often combine these tricks.

Slope-style courses have flat areas, jumps, and moguls. Moguls are a series of mounds made of snow. Boarders do as many tricks as they can in each area. They receive more points for difficult tricks like handstands and flips. Boarders also receive points for speed.

Boarders do half-pipe tricks on slope-style courses, too. On mogul areas, a boarder may do some ollies. The boarder may do a tailgrab while in the air. On flat areas, a boarder may do a fakie in combination with other tricks.

In freestyle events, riders receive points for doing tricks. Judges give the boarders more points for difficult tricks. Boarders lose points for going too slow, not doing tricks well, or falling down.

Downhill Events

During downhill events, boarders race one another on a course. A downhill course runs along a mountain slope. It has wide and sharp curves. It also has straight areas where boarders gain speed.

There are two downhill events. The first event is a speed race. In a speed race, boarders race through a downhill course. Some boarders go as fast as 70 miles (112 kilometers) per hour. Boarders try to complete the course in the shortest time.

The slalom race is the second event. For a slalom race, poles are set up along a downhill course. Boarders must race in and out between the poles. Some slalom boarders reach speeds of 50 to 60 miles (80 to 96 kilometers) per hour. They try to finish a course in the least amount of time.

Boarders lose speed and time if they hit poles. Boarders are out of the race if they skip a pole or fall.

Chapter 4

The Newest Competitions

Today's extreme snowboarding competitions also include new events. Boarders looking for new challenges have helped create these events. These events include big air and boardercross competitions.

Recently, snowboarding became an Olympic sport, too. The Olympic Games are a series of sports contests between athletes from many countries. Countries organize teams of their best athletes in each sport.

Big Air

Big air competitions are exciting to watch. Big air means a high, long jump into the air. In big air competitions, boarders ride their boards off

Big air competitions feature high, long jumps into the air.

Moguls are located between turns on a boardercross course.

jumps. The jumps shoot boarders high into
the air.

The riders do tricks while in midair. These
tricks are often the same as those performed in
slope-style and half-pipe competitions. Other
tricks include spins and somersaults. Judges give
boarders points based on how well they do tricks.
They also give boarders points for how exciting
their tricks are.

Boardercross

Boardercross events feature as many as six racers competing on a challenging course. The boarder who finishes the race first wins. The course has a series of right and left turns. These turns are called burms. The burms increase each boarder's speed.

Jumps and moguls are located between each burm. Boarders hit the jumps and moguls at high speeds. Boarders must control their speed and balance as they go through the course. Many boarders crash into one another and fall. Boarders who fall down usually cannot win the race.

The Extreme Games

The Extreme Games are a series of competitions featuring many extreme sports. The games are shown on television. Extreme snowboarding is one of the featured sports. The Extreme Games are also called the X Games.

There are Summer and Winter X Games. Snowboarding is part of the Winter X Games. Extreme boarders compete to win $200,000 or more in prize money.

Many boarders find it difficult to finish the steep courses at Crested Butte ski area.

The snowboarding events are slope-style, half-pipe, big air, and boardercross. In the X Games, boardercross is called boarder X.

The Olympics

Snowboarding is now an Olympic sport. Men and women boarders have the chance to compete. But boarders are limited to slalom racing and half-pipe riding.

Boarders hope the Olympics will feature more snowboarding events in the future. They hope that downhill, big air, and boardercross boarders will also be included. This would give more boarders a chance to compete.

Other Competitions

There are two big snowboarding competitions in North America every year. The first is the United States Extreme Snowboarding Championships. This competition takes place at Crested Butte. Crested Butte is a ski area in Colorado.

Crested Butte has many snowboarding courses. It features several steep downhill courses. The courses have drop-offs of 30 to 40 feet (9 to 12 meters).

The courses also have natural dangers such as rocks and rocky passages. Boarders have a difficult time on these courses. Many boarders find it difficult to finish the harder courses.

The best boarders receive cash and a round-trip ticket to Valdez, Alaska. There, they race in the World Extreme Championship. The winners earn the titles King and Queen of the Hill. Boarders consider the winners among the best snowboarders in the world.

Chapter 5
Equipment

Extreme snowboarding requires very little equipment. A snowboarder needs a board, boots, bindings, and warm clothing. A binding is a device that attaches a boarder's boot to a board.

The Board

Most snowboards are made of laminates. A laminate is layers of wood strips glued together. Laminate boards are strong. They last longer than boards made of plastics or single pieces of wood. Some new boards have a combination of laminates and man-made elements.

There are four types of snowboards. Each type of board is best for certain kinds of snowboarding. Extreme boarders believe that the correct board makes their ride faster, easier, and safer.

A snowboarder needs a board, boots, bindings, and warm clothing.

Extreme boards are strong and stiff to withstand jumps off cliffs and drop-offs.

Freestyle and Freeride Boards

The first kind of board is the freestyle board. It is meant for slower riding. The freestyle board has more flexibility than other boards. Flexibility is the ability of a snowboard to bend. Flexibility gives a boarder more control over speed and tricks. A freestyle board works well for half-pipes and on firmly packed snow.

The freeride board is the second kind of board. It is narrower than many other boards. This allows a boarder to make quick turns. A freeride board works well in powder and for doing tricks.

Race Boards and Extreme Boards

The third kind of board is the race board. It is much longer and narrower than other boards. It is made to travel lightly across the snow. This helps a boarder go faster. Race boards are best for downhill events.

The fourth kind of board is the extreme board. It is strong and narrow but does not have much flexibility. The strength and stiffness of the board allow it to withstand jumps off cliffs or drop-offs. The board's narrowness gives a boarder better control for tight turns. Narrowness also makes the board fast. These features make the board work well for backcountry snowboarding.

Bindings

There are several types of snowboard bindings. Most bindings have two or three straps. Boarders use the straps to attach their boots to their snowboards. Some bindings also have stiff, high backs that help support boarders' lower legs and ankles.

Extreme downhill boarders wear hard boots.

The newest type of bindings are step-ins. Step-in bindings are devices that allow boarders to step into their bindings. Step-in bindings release boarders' boots during a crash. This keeps the boarders' legs and ankles from twisting or breaking.

Some bindings are adjustable. Adjustable bindings let boarders change how tightly their boots fit onto their boards. Beginners need a tight fit. This helps them control their boards. Extreme boarders often adjust the fit. They do this to help them perform different tricks.

Boots

Snowboarding boots come in hard and soft styles. Most extreme snowboarders wear soft boots. Soft boots vary in their firmness and flexibility.

Beginners usually need firmer, less flexible soft boots. These boots keep boarders' ankles straight. This helps prevent new boarders from twisting their ankles.

Extreme freestyle boarders also wear soft boots. They usually wear softer, more flexible soft boots. The boots are light and bend easily so boarders' ankles can move freely. This allows freestyle boarders to perform their tricks. Some backcountry boarders wear soft boots, too.

Extreme boarders use hard boots for downhill snowboarding. The boots give them more control on steep courses, firmly packed snow, and icy slopes. Some backcountry boarders also wear hard boots.

Some extreme boarders wear helmets and ski goggles.

Helmets

Many extreme downhill boarders wear helmets.
Wearing helmets is one of the rules of the sport.
Helmets protect boarders' heads. Extreme
boarders know that falls and crashes can
be dangerous.

There are many types of helmets but they all have the same basic features. Snowboarding helmets are small and light. They cover the head but not the face or eyes. Boarders decide which helmets are best for them.

Clothing and Goggles

Extreme snowboarders wear clothes that are comfortable, warm, and dry. Their clothes are loose to give them free movement. Free movement helps boarders race and perform tricks.

Many extreme boarders wear specially made clothing. Sometimes they wear water resistant jackets and pants. Water resistant clothing takes longer to become wet. Some boarders wear snowboarding pants. The pants keep out water. They also have padding that helps cushion boarders during falls.

Many extreme boarders wear ski goggles or sunglasses. Ski goggles are protective glasses that fit tightly around the upper face and eyes. Ski goggles and sunglasses keep snow out of boarders' eyes.

Hat and Sunglasses

Water Resistant Jacket

Water Resistant Pants

Gloves

Boots and Bindings

Snowboard

Chapter 6
Dangers and Safety

Extreme snowboarding can be dangerous. It requires a high level of skill and extra safety. Beginners should not try extreme snowboarding until they learn the basics. Ski areas and snow parks often have instructors to help beginners learn the sport.

Extreme boarders learn and practice many skills. This helps make them become better at their sport. They keep practicing the skills they have already mastered. Extreme boarders know that laziness can mean getting hurt.

There are three common extreme snowboarding dangers. Extreme backcountry boarding has additional dangers. All extreme boarders know the dangers of the sport. But they learn how to protect themselves. They also learn when to seek treatment.

Extreme snowboarding requires high levels of skill and safety.

Many extreme boarders wear warm clothing, hats, and gloves to prevent hypothermia.

Hypothermia

One snowboarding danger is hypothermia. Hypothermia occurs when the body's temperature falls below 91 degrees Fahrenheit (33 degrees Celsius). A person's normal body temperature is about 98.6 degrees Fahrenheit (37 degrees Celsius). People can die if the body does not return to its normal temperature.

Extreme boarders know the signs of hypothermia. Early signs include chills and shivers that will not stop. Other signs include arms and legs that do not move right. Later signs of hypothermia are sleepiness and bewilderment. Extreme boarders quit boarding if they have any of these signs. They seek warmth and medical treatment.

To prevent hypothermia, extreme boarders eat well before they snowboard. Eating well gives them energy and helps them stay warm. They wear warm, dry clothing. Warm dry clothing also holds in body heat. Many boarders wear hats or headbands to hold in body heat.

Dehydration

Dehydration is another danger for snowboarders. Dehydration occurs when the body loses too much water. Water helps the body keep its normal temperature. It also helps the heart and other organs work properly. Dehydration can lead to frostbite, hypothermia, or death.

Sweating is one way the body can become dehydrated. Extreme boarders know they must drink plenty of water. This replaces the water lost through sweating. Extreme boarders drink water even if they are not thirsty. This helps prevent dehydration.

An avalanche is one of the biggest dangers in extreme backcountry snowboarding.

Frostbite

Snowboarders also run the risk of frostbite. Frostbite occurs when cold air freezes uncovered skin or skin next to wet clothing. Minor frostbite is not deadly, but it is painful. Major frostbite can lead to the loss of frostbitten body parts. Boarders can also die from severe frostbite.

An early sign of frostbite is a tingling feeling in uncovered skin. Later signs include a burning feeling or loss of feeling in the frostbitten areas.

Extreme boarders prevent frostbite by covering as much of their skin as possible. They wear warm, dry clothing. They wear gloves to protect their hands. They also wear hats to protect their ears.

Extreme boarders quit boarding at the first sign of frostbite. They treat minor frostbitten areas with warm water. Boarders seek medical help for treatment of severely frostbitten areas.

Avalanche

Extreme backcountry boarders learn and practice mountain climbing skills. They carry mountain climbing tools. They learn about snow and weather dangers.

An avalanche is one of the biggest dangers for backcountry boarders. An avalanche is a large mass of snow and ice that suddenly slides down the side of a mountain. Unstable snow causes an avalanche. Unstable means not firm or steady. Temperature changes make the snow unstable.

People who do not know about unstable snow can start an avalanche. They might do this by hiking, skiing, or snowboarding on the snow. Sometimes loud noises such as gun shots can start an avalanche.

Boarders know that they can be covered by deep snow during an avalanche. Deep snow can crush a boarder. A boarder could suffocate under just a few

Extreme backcountry boarders never snowboard alone.

feet (meters) of snow. Suffocate means to die from lack of air.

Conditions and Safety Measures

Backcountry boarders always check the snow and weather before they snowboard. They listen to weather reports and avalanche reports. These reports tell boarders about dangerous weather and areas of unstable snow.

Backcountry boarders never snowboard alone. They snowboard with at least one other person. Many times, they snowboard in groups. This way the boarders can keep track of one another. They can also help one another if problems occur.

Backcountry boarders carry avalanche equipment. The equipment includes two-way radios. A two-way radio allows two or more people to talk to each other. This is important if boarders are separated or an accident happens.

Backcountry boarders also carry small shovels, food, water, and probes. A probe is a long, thin pole that can folded up. Boarders use probes to find group members who are buried in the snow.

A Safe Future

Extreme boarders are working hard to make their sport safer. They continue to learn new safety skills. Snowboard manufacturers are making equipment that meets the needs of the boarders. Together, boarders and manufacturers are making extreme snowboarding safe for today and the future.

Words to Know

athlete (ATH-leet)—someone trained in a sport or game

avalanche (AV-uh-lanch)—a large mass of snow and ice that suddenly slides down the side of a mountain

big air (BIG AIR)—a high, long jump into the air

binding (BINE-ding)—a device or straps that attach a boarder's boot to a snowboard

competition (kom-puh-TISH-uhn)—a contest between two or more athletes

dehydration (dee-hye-DRAY-shun)—when the body loses too much water

downhill (DOUN-hill)—a snowboarding competition featuring speed and slalom events

Extreme Games (ek-STREEM GAMES)—a series of competitions featuring many extreme sports; also known as the X Games

flexibility (flex-suh-BIL-i-tee) —the ability of a snowboard to bend

freestyle (FREE-stile)—snowboarding event featuring half-pipe and slope-style riding

frostbite (FRAWST-bite)—when cold air freezes uncovered skin or skin next to wet clothing

half-pipe (HAF-pipe)—a U-shaped freestyle course in the snow with high walls

hypothermia (hye-puh-THUR-mee-uh)—when body temperature falls below 91 degrees Fahrenheit (33 degrees Celsius)

laminate (LAM-uh-nuht)—layers of wood strips glued together

probe (PROHB)—a long, thin pole that can be poked into the snow to help find a buried person

ski goggles (SKEE GOG-uhlz)—protective glasses that fit tightly around the upper face and eyes

slalom (SLAH-luhm)—a downhill event where boarders race in and out between poles

snowboard (SNOH-bord)—a laminate, plastic, or wooden board that looks like a large snow ski

snow park (SNOH PARK)—an area set aside for snowboarders at ski areas

Snurfer (SNURF-ur)—the first snowboard; invented by Sherman Poppen in the mid 1960s

To Learn More

Althen, K.C. *The Complete Book of Snowboarding.* Rutland, Vt.: Charles E. Tuttle, 1990.

Bennett, Jeff and Scott Downey. *The Complete Snowboarder*. Camden, Maine: Ragged Mountain Press, 1994.

Brimner, Larry Dane. *Snowboarding*. New York: Franklin Watts, 1990.

Lurie, Jon. *Fundamental Snowboarding*. Minneapolis: Lerner Publications, 1996.

McMullen, J. *Basic Essentials of Snowboarding*. Merrillville, Ind.: ICS Books, 1991.

Tomlinson, Joe. *Extreme Sports: The Illustrated Guide to Maximum Adrenaline Thrills*. New York: Smithmark Publishers, 1996.

Useful Addresses

Canadian Snowboard Federation
30-1507 West 12th Avenue
Vancouver, BC V6J 2E2
Canada

International Snowboarding Federation
ISF Worldwide Services
Pradlerstrasse 21
Innsbruck, Austria A-6020

U.S. Snowboarding
Box 100
Park City, UT 84060

United States of America Snowboard Association (USASA)
315 E. Alcott Avenue
Fergus Falls, MN 56537

Internet Sites

ESPNET SportsZone: Extreme Games
http://espnet.sportszone.com/editors/xgames/
   index.html

The ISF Homepage
http://www.isf.ch

Snowboarding Online
http://www.solsnowboarding.com/index.html

**United States of America Snowboard
Association (USASA)**
http://www.usasa.org

**Extreme boarders keep practicing skills they have
already mastered.**

Index